# ALL ABOUT CHIRON

## in Houses, Signs and Aspects

### by Maritha Pottenger

Number 15          $4.95

## ASTRONOMICAL BACKGROUND

Chiron has been called a planetoid (small planet), and an asteroid [#2060] (although most asteroids orbit in the Asteroid Belt between Mars and Jupiter). Currently, some astronomers theorize that Chiron is a former comet. We do know that it is a small body (180 kilometers in diameter) which orbits between Jupiter and Uranus. (Because Chiron's orbit is so elliptical, we cannot say it orbits only between Saturn and Uranus.) Chiron was discovered by Charles Kowal in 1977, so astrologers have had a limited period of time to study its significance in horoscopes. Chiron orbits the zodiac in about 50 years. Due to Chiron's irregular orbit, it spends a relatively long time in certain signs (Capricorn, Aquarius, Pisces, Aries and Taurus) and moves relatively quickly through others (Gemini through Sagittarius).

Astrologers were given access to an ephemeris of Chiron within a year or two of its discovery. Chiron ephemerides were published by both Al H. Morrison's *CAO Times* and by Malcolm Dean. Zane Stein provided some of the first in-depth studies of Chiron through his Association for the Study of Chiron. Several books have been written by Stein and others, despite the relatively brief time since discovery.

## MYTHOLOGICAL BACKGROUND

Many astrologers have noted that the names given to minor bodies (such as asteroids) appear to be "right" — that is, the mythology or associations of the names seem to fit. Chiron, in the Greek myth, was a centaur — half man, half horse. He was noted as a teacher of heroes. He taught Hercules, for example. Chiron also taught Aesculapius, who taught Hippocrates, who was the father of modern medicine. One of Chiron's students accidentally wounded Chiron. Being immortal, Chiron could not die, but he suffered great pain from his wound. Zeus (Jupiter) took pity upon Chiron and turned him into the constellation Sagittarius.

## ASTROLOGICAL ASSOCIATIONS

The myth suggests a clear association of Chiron with Sagittarius. Some astrologers have emphasized the "wounded healer" persona of the mythology and suggest Virgo or other health/healing connections. My experience is that the Sagittarius connection fits very well. If we consider that the driving thrust of Sagittarius is a search for ultimate truth, spiritual (and physical) healing could be one of the focuses in a quest for total truth. The Sagittarius association also brings in education, travel, spiritual quests, religion, or anything which expands our mental and/or physical horizons. There is a restless, seeking, searching quality to Sagittarius.

In the natural zodiac, Sagittarius falls in the 9th house, so we understand the urge to seek the best, the highest, the most ideal. This idealistic thrust can be a problem if we promise more than we can deliver, or look for godlike perfection from areas of life which involve mere human beings. Jupiter, Sagittarius, and the 9th house (and, presumably, Chiron) can point to areas where we expect more than is possible, where we may overidealize (and be disappointed) or continually expand — seeking more and more and **more** of whatever we define as an ultimate good. Chiron thus relates to beliefs, values and ideals.

Sagittarius also has a strong theme of freedom, as one needs a degree of independence in order to seek Truth and ultimate Goodness. ("Good-bye, I'm off to Tibet to seek enlightenment.")

## KEY WORDS

The following are some suggested key words for Chiron: drive for knowledge, thirst for enlightenment, ideals, maverick, truth-seeking, teacher/student/ healer, urge to know **more**, pioneer, quest for perfection, urge to go beyond known boundaries, optimistic, worship, trust, value, drive to experiment/ take risks, freedom needs.

## EXAMPLES

### Educational Emphasis

There was the woman born with Chiron on the Ascendant. Her family was only into "beer drinking and horse racing" according to her. She felt driven, from an early age, to go to the library, to study, to learn. Her family laughed at her, but she felt this intense inner desire to learn, especially through books.

Another woman born with Chiron rising said: "When my friends see me after we haven't been together for awhile, they do not ask 'How are you?' They ask, 'What are you studying now?'"

Among students who attend our 10-day Astrology Intensives in Helena, Montana each year, there is often a strong Chiron — on an angle, conjunct the Sun, Moon, Mars, Ascendant ruler, etc. They are willing to devote a lot of time, energy, and money to seeking the truth, particularly spiritual answers.

### Idealism

Several clients with Chiron in the 7th have expected a lot in relationships. One individual with a strong freedom focus in her chart is still unmarried at age 40 (no one ever was quite ideal enough), although she is seeing a Sagittarian at the moment. It is particularly worth watching clients born in the mid-1940s when Jupiter, Neptune, and Chiron (all associated with the quest for the infinite, seeking God in some fashion) were in Libra (partnership). For some periods, Juno (the marriage asteroid) was conjunct Jupiter, Neptune or Chiron. The post-war generation was most affected by psychoanalysis and the decline of traditional religion. Psychology, having no spiritual basis, tended to overemphasize relationships. People were encouraged to expect husbands and wives to be best friends, sexually exciting, mentally stimulating, good providers and a whole host of other qualities that are more than one person can generally provide. Many people ended up expecting more than is humanly possible of themselves, of their partners, and of their personal relationships. The divorce rate rose among this generation and continued to rise.

Jupiter, Neptune and Chiron also traveled through Scorpio, which is related to sexuality and the desire for a mate with whom to share money, resources and pleasures. The Scorpio sojourn was not shared by Jupiter, Neptune and Chiron. There was a period in the late 1950s when Jupiter was in Scorpio, while Neptune was still in Libra, but Chiron was in Aquarius. In parts of 1969 and 1970, Jupiter was in Libra and Scorpio while Neptune was in Scorpio (but Chiron occupied Aries). These Jupiter and Neptune placements again focus on idealization, or seeking the absolute in relationships. Naturally, the constructive form of Jupiter/Neptune/Chiron in Libra/Scorpio would be choosing partners (and relationships) who emphasize mental stimulation, the quest for the truth, searching, mysticism, individuality, and moral and ethical principles. People can stay together when they share similar beliefs, goals and values, so long as neither one expects the other to be already perfect — able to provide total happiness.

Chiron in an earth house ties the ideals to making a living. Several clients with Chiron in the 6th or 10th have searched for that perfect, ideal job, or tried to do their work to meet an infinite standard. Especially with other mutability in the horoscopes, the individuals can be job hoppers, each time hoping the next position will be "**the**" one.

Other clients have managed to find a job which makes a more ideal world, such as therapists, nuns, priests, etc. Or, they have found careers which involve the pursuit of knowledge (teaching) or disseminating information or inspiration to others (writing and publishing). For example, in Barbara Hand Clow's book, *Chiron*, she gives example charts of three publishers.

One has Chiron in Taurus in the 2nd (earning money through the mind and ideals). The second has Chiron in Sagittarius in the 10th house of career. The third has Chiron conjunct Pluto (which rules the Midheaven). Ms. Clow also includes a writer who has Neptune conjunct Jupiter conjunct Chiron in Libra in the 2nd. Of the five priests, nuns or theologians Ms. Clow includes, two have Chiron in the 10th; one has Chiron in the 2nd. The fourth has Chiron rising in Sagittarius (but a 9th house stellium including the Midheaven ruler and Neptune in the 10th strongly tie ideals to career). The fifth individual has Chiron in the 7th (married to God) along with Neptune conjunct the Midheaven and Jupiter conjunct the Sun in the 2nd.

## Optimism
One client with a Cancer stellium (in the 3rd and 4th houses) but Chiron conjunct her Taurus Ascendant emphasized: "I am **always** up. I'm definitely an optimist, and most astrologers have read my chart as moody and depressive. That's not me!"

## Travel
One woman with Chiron on the Ascendant was born in Europe, but has traveled constantly throughout her life. One man with Chiron conjunct Mercury writes humor and loves to travel (short and long trips).

# INTERPRETATIONS
The above is perhaps enough to give the reader some idea. This section will provide brief delineations of Chiron by sign, house, and aspect (along with a few examples of famous people).

As with any relatively slow (outer planet) body, the sign placements are less personal than the house placements. Similarly, aspects involving outer planets could hold for quite a number of births, while aspects to inner planets tends to reflect more individual, personal issues.

# CHIRON IN THE HOUSES
## CHIRON IN 1ST HOUSE
You probably expect a lot of yourself. You may be quite idealistic, eager to learn, spiritual, ethical, religious, philosophical, or perennially seeking **more** out of life. You might fall into the extremes of "I am perfect" (overrating self), or "I should be perfect" (demanding more than is reasonable of yourself). You may be a perpetual student, teacher, traveller, and seeker of truth — **or** believe you personally have the ultimate answers (and take a guru role). Your principles are your very own and quite personal.

You can experiment with different ways of expressing yourself. Original thinking is probably instinctive for you. You could generalize about assertion, anger, or self-expression and might rethink or revolutionize ideas about courage, identity, or crises. You tend to be optimistic, easily focusing on the positive in life. You are apt to be future-oriented.

Your personal actions are affected by the big picture. Your identity may be connected to group consciousness. Democratic ideals probably come naturally to you. You are usually direct and straightforward in your perception of individual truths.

**Examples:** *Rollo May, Paramahansa Yogananda, Norman Mailer, Karl Marx, R.D. Laing, H.G. Wells, Konrad Adenauer, W.B. Yeats.*

## CHIRON IN 2ND HOUSE

You may expect a lot sensually, materially or financially. You could turn money, pleasure, indulgence or comfort into an ultimate value — and seek it perennially (amassing more and more) *or* be dissatisfied that you never have enough. Alternatively, you may earn money and get pleasure through seeking ultimate truth — fields such as education, religion, publishing, or anything which is idealistic or expands mental and physical horizons. Your principles are important in your handling of material goods, gains and gratifications. You may find comfort in individual truths or a spiritual path.

You can experiment in your handling of pleasures, possessions and tangible forms. You might generalize about physical gratification and money. You may do some very original thinking about security, comfort, resources, beauty, and satisfaction. You could examine ideas and ideals about ownership, salaries, aesthetics, or the physical senses. The big picture might influence your finances, pleasures, and possessions. Your income (and outgo) could be affected by group consciousness. Democratic principles probably appeal where pleasure and tangibles are concerned.

**Examples:** *David Bowie, Walter Mondale, Benjamin Disraeli, Cat Stevens, Jack Paar, Alice Cooper, Victor Hugo, Alan Watts.*

## CHIRON IN 3RD HOUSE

You may expect a lot of siblings, relatives or the mind. Original thinking permeates your mental style. Your mind, tongue and hands (dexterity) could be quick and versatile. You are apt to idealize thinking, communication, learning, variety, flexibility, or perception. You may expect more than is possible of yourself in the intellectual arena. ("I should always know the right answers.") You may idealize understanding, versatility, the mind, or objectivity. Or, your principles may be adaptable and changeable (situationally-based). You can see many sides to individual truth.

You know how to experiment with words and information. You can be adroit at reforming ideas. You easily generalize in your learning and teaching. You may seek information about the big picture, especially ultimate truths — religion, philosophy, spiritual quests, etc. Group consciousness could affect your intellectual world. Both learning and teaching come easily to you. You may value equal access to information — trying to democratize the flow of knowledge in the world. You tend to believe that the mind can handle anything — that ultimate solutions lie in thinking and communicating.

Idealism could be a theme with siblings or other relatives. You might idealize a family member (putting them up on a pedestal). Your values, principles, and world view are likely to be strongly influenced by a sibling, relative or teacher. You may expect more than is reasonable of those around you — or feel you cannot measure up to their high standards. Alternatively, you encourage your relatives to manifest their highest potentials and they help you aim for the best as well.

**Examples:** *Phil Donahue, Arlo Guthrie, Yehudi Menuhin, Sandy Koufax, Robert Redford, Edgar Degas, Paul Gauguin, Sigmund Freud, Jean-Paul Sartre.*

## CHIRON IN 4TH HOUSE

You tend to expect a lot of your mother, your own mothering, home or family. Your mother figure could be religious, idealistic, optimistic, involved with foreign lands, intellectual, have high standards, or chronically want **more** from life. Your nurturing parent influenced your ideas and ideals — what you define as ultimate truth in life. (Her beliefs may be a positive example you emulate — or a negative one, in which case you move in the opposite direction.) Your principles are affected by your family roots.

You are apt to place a high value on your home — wanting to create the ideal nest — but not wanting to stay there! You may have a home on the road, in a foreign country, with lots of people coming and going, a religious or spiritual home, or a home full of books, interesting people, and fascinating discussions. Group consciousness may be illuminated in your home and you might even have a communal situation. You could bring the wider world into your home (or take your home into the world). You may feel torn between security and safety — valuing rootedness, but seeking variety in the domestic realm. You could place a high value on your homeland and be quite patriotic or concerned with the course of your country.

You can experiment with emotions, dependency and nurturance needs, and domestic arrangements. You may think, theorize and experiment about feelings. You may feel torn between intellect and emotions, between attachment and separation. Your relationship with a nurturing figure could have been ambivalent — unsure how much you wanted closeness and how much you wanted to be independent. Your mothering figure was probably working on the balance between emotional connections and the independence to explore the wider world. If she overdid either side, you would tend to take on the opposite.

You are likely to want to nurture in an ideal fashion, and may demand more than is reasonable of yourself in that realm — or avoid caretaking for fear of not doing it perfectly. Your challenge is to come to terms with your early experience of mothering (whether too much independence or too much closeness or a good balance) and seek the best in your own expression (while still allowing yourself to be human and fallible). You can nurture ideas and be emotionally supportive of idealism.

**Examples:** *Zubin Mehta, Ernest Hemingway, Bill Moyers, Hal Holbrook, Helen Reddy, John Denver, John H. Glenn, Nelson Rockefeller.*

## CHIRON IN 5TH HOUSE

You may expect a lot of those you love, and of love itself. You could turn romance, children, love, creativity, sex, or a starring role into an ultimate value. If you overidealize any of the above, you may want more and more and be insatiable (romantically, sexually, in being onstage, etc.). If you seek only the best, you may avoid a part of life rather than having something less ideal (e.g., not have children, not get romantically involved, etc.). The middle ground allows you to encourage the best in those you love — praising, motivating, and egging them on in terms of ideas and ideals. Their views would also affect your principles, values or moral attitudes. You can feed each other's excitement and joy in seeking the highest in life.

You could experiment creatively, with a zest for change. You can generalize about joy, drama and expansive potentials. You may reform ideas about speculation, risk-taking, thrills, or fun. You can get excited by individual truth. You probably embrace, admire, and approve of original thinking. You are apt to perceive democratic ideals as generous, superior and exciting. You are working on the balance between group consciousness and your need to be special. You can infuse light, life and charisma into the big picture.

**Examples:** *John F. Kennedy, John Lennon, Ringo Starr, Henry Miller, John Derek, James Dean, John C. Fremont, Arnold Schwarzenegger.*

## CHIRON IN 6TH HOUSE

You may expect a lot of colleagues, your job, or yourself as a worker. You might seek the perfect job (and could be chronically dissatisfied or a job-hopper). You might try to do your work perfectly (and demand that you never make a mistake). You might make work your ultimate value in life, the area where you put your trust and look for meaning — which risks a loss of faith if you lose a job. You might find work which makes a more perfect, or a more ideal, ethical, or spiritual world. Your job could contribute to the betterment of people or society. You could pursue democratic ideals at work. Group consciousness might affect your work place or routines on the job. You might work in a field involving travel, education, religion, teaching, publishing, or anything inspirational. You might work with your mind, or original thinking could contribute to your productivity.

Your principles are apt to be practical, organized and logical. You may believe that the big picture calls for patience, thoroughness, and service. You may subject individual truth to critical investigation. You can rethink and reform ideas through analysis, discrimination and flaw-finding. You want to put the mind to work in the world, so experiment with ideas and ideals practically, measuringly, with a drive for useful applications.

You may generalize about work, health or common sense. You could idealize good health, or seek perfect physical functioning. You might be widely read concerning matters of health, nutrition, hygiene or bodily well-being. You probably place a high value on being competent in the body and on the job.

**Examples:** *Dr. Tom Dooley, Louis Pasteur, Dustin Hoffman, Albert Camus, Johnny Carson, Elvis Presley, Auguste Rodin, Clint Eastwood.*

## CHIRON IN 7TH HOUSE

You probably expect a lot of a partner, of marriage, or of yourself as a partner. Outcomes can range from avoiding marriage (if you cannot do it perfectly), to putting a partner on a pedestal (and being disappointed if s/he falls off), to adopting guru/student roles, to expecting a relationship to be "everything" to you, to constantly looking for someone new, exciting, or more ideal in your relationships. You might overrate other people. If you feel threatened by their potential abilities or intelligence, you might strive to "prove" your superiority. Or, you can attract bright, idealistic, optimistic people who emphasize goals, values and the quest for knowledge. Allowing others to search for truth in their own individual ways is vital, but shared values will greatly aid your partnership(s). You can experiment in roles with other people, and may reform ideas about people, interactions or beauty. Your original thinking can contribute to your ability to negotiate and harmonize.

You can make generalizations about sharing, harmony and balance. You usually believe that the big picture calls for grace, charm, equality, and cooperation — though the 7th house can also manifest as competition.

Democratic ideals are preferred in your one-to-one encounters. Your principles often relate to seeing both sides and balancing polarities. You place a high value on justice and fair play.

**Examples:** *Upton Sinclair, William Holden, Stephen Foster, Benito Mussolini, Claude Debussy, Prince Andrew, George Moscone, Ellen Burstyn, Bob Dylan.*

## CHIRON IN 8TH HOUSE

You may expect a lot of a mate, of intimacy, or of yourself as a mate. You could idealize sexuality, resources, pleasures, or deep, psychological insights. You might give any of them too much importance, pursuing more and more in your life. Or, you might expect more than is possible from your mate, from close connections, or from yourself as an intimate partner. Accepting the humanity of people close to you, rather than seeking perfection, may be a challenge.

If you are still looking for the "supreme" emotional high, you may experiment with sexuality, shared finances, or intimate exchanges. You might pioneer, speculate and take risks in these areas. You are learning to balance individual freedom and truths with your desire to merge with another person. You may feel torn between the independence to pursue knowledge (particularly about psychological complexes and hidden motives) versus the desire for a total emotional commitment. You could reform ideas about sharing and transform your relationships. Original thinking can contribute to your capacity to give, receive, and share equally with others.

Your principles are apt to be deeply felt (perhaps a bit fanatic at times?) and influence others. You may value power, potency, intensity, perseverance, and forcefulness. Being in charge might be given too much significance and meaning. You are working on the balance between democratic ideals and a drive for power. Heavy conflict patterns could indicate lessons in these areas. Self-mastery and self-control could be significant goals for you. You can generalize about psychological complexes and hidden motives. Your quest for insights includes both breadth and depth.

**Examples:** *H.R. Haldeman, Otto von Bismarck, Jack Kerouac, Kaiser Wilhelm II, John Gacy, Jack Nicklaus, Martin Luther, Joe Frazier.*

## CHIRON IN 9TH HOUSE

You tend to expect a lot from justice, education or travel. You might turn individual truth into an absolute, believe in looking on the positive, place a high value on the mind, or be constantly driven to seek answers about the meaning of life. You can experiment with world views, philosophies and ideas. Your thinking about answers can be quite original, creative and pioneering. You may periodically reform your ideas about life's meaning.

You might generalize about religion, beliefs or values. Your principles probably include honesty, generosity, fairness. Democratic ideals may be among your ultimate values. You can be original in your thinking about truth and ethics.

You're probably a natural seeker, looking for ultimate answers through philosophy, science, religion, spiritual quests, education, travel, or anything which expands your horizons. Or, you could turn speculation, expansion, risk-taking, good times, or humor into an ultimate value — seeking more and more. Group consciousness might influence your moral principles and ethical ideas. You tend to be optimistic about the big picture and usually believe that the future will be brighter than the past.

**Examples:** *Enrico Fermi, George Bernard Shaw, Burl Ives, Warren Beatty, Edouard Manet, Philip Berrigan, Galileo, F. Nietzsche.*

## CHIRON IN 10TH HOUSE

You are likely to expect a lot from your career, your professional role, or authority figures. You may want the ideal vocation, perhaps being too restless to settle down into anything less than perfect. Or, you may idealize the work ethic, believing that doing a good job and achieving success is an ultimate value. Or, you may work toward making a more ideal world, in fields such as writing, publishing, the law, theology, etc. Group consciousness may play a role in your ambitions and attainments. You probably set high standards for achievement. Your individual perception of truth may contribute to your career.

Your beliefs and values are apt to be influenced by a father or authority figure. If you got along with that individual, your principles are probably parallel. If you did not get along, your beliefs are probably the exact reverse. You may have seen authorities (or power) as idealized (and be disappointed when they turned out to be human). You may give too much significance to power, mastery and control. Your sense of faith and trust, your optimism about the universe, are strongly affected by mentors and power people. Your challenge is to clarify your individual understanding of power and its limits, yet remain able to easily relate to authority figures, and to work within life's rules.

Your seeking of the truth is apt to be responsible. You want to bring ideals down to earth, make them useful in the world. Your principles highlight respect, capability and strength. You could generalize about karma, experience, reality; you are seeking universal rules and law. You may experiment with guilt, protocols and different structures. Your quest for answers tends to be very purposeful and serious. You could reform ideas about limits, laws, and lessons. You learn much through experience.

**Examples:** *Alfred Tennyson, Michel Gauquelin, Adolf Eichman, Jack Anderson, Jerry Rubin, Heinrich Himmler, Sam Peckinpah, Robert McNamara.*

## CHIRON IN 11TH HOUSE

You may expect a lot from your friends, friendship or humanitarian principles. You might put acquaintances up on pedestals and feel disappointed when they are only human. Or, you may turn friendship into an ultimate value, seeking more and more. Or, you could be drawn to idealistic organizations. You are apt to emphasize democratic ideals in your interactions with others. You tend to believe each person has his/her own individual truth. Your thinking can be quite original, revolutionary, defiant and insightful.

You may experiment in groups, causes, organizations and associations. Your principles are probably humanitarian, equalitarian, open-ended and a bit unusual. You see much change and flux in life. You are always ready to reform ideas, adding your own unique twist. Group consciousness may influence your thinking, values, and perceptions. You can generalize about freedom, the masses, equality or the new age. The freedom to go beyond traditional boundaries — in thinking, in friendship, and in a pull toward the future — is essential to you.

**Examples:** *Tom Smothers, Merv Griffin, O. Henry, Lawrence Welk, Gregory Peck, Arthur Ashe, Albert Einstein, Jules Verne, Jack London.*

## CHIRON IN 12TH HOUSE

You could expect a lot from God, nature, compassion or intuition. You might overvalue mystical experiences or nonverbal knowing (perhaps to the point of gullibility). You may believe strongly in compassion, perhaps to the point of savior/victim entanglements. You have a strong streak of idealism, which is probably partly unconscious. Your principles are cosmic, romantic, transcendent. You may touch the infinite through art, nature, or beauty. You could place a very high value on grace, harmony, compassion or anything aesthetic (painting, poetry, singing, writing, etc.). You may experiment with cosmic consciousness and altered states. You can generalize about faith, trust, union and art. You can make original contributions in terms of mysticism, spirituality, art, or healing and helping activities. You can blend the head and heart.

The big picture, in your eyes, is interconnected; separation is an illusion. Democratic ideals pervade your experience of the universe and a Higher Power. Group consciousness may influence your charitable instincts and desire to assist. In your eyes, individual truths are easily dissolved, idealized or transcendent. You may reform ideas with sensitivity, deception or clairvoyance.

**Examples:** *Maurice Chevalier, Ernie Pyle, Harry Belafonte, Dorothy Hamill, Fred Astaire, Abraham Lincoln, Walt Whitman, Ada Byron.*

## CHIRON IN SIGNS

### CHIRON IN ARIES

You seek the truth assertively, spontaneously, and naturally. You instinctively learn and teach. Your idealism is personal. You can be a maverick and need to go beyond known boundaries. You may be physically restless and active, or just constantly on the move with your mind. Optimistic, you are willing to experiment and to take risks. The freedom to do and know **more** is important to you.

**Examples:** *Jackie Robinson, Sir Richard Burton (explorer), Steve Allen, Copernicus, Michelangelo, Machiavelli, Kepler, Kant, Winston Churchill, Peter Sellers.*

### CHIRON IN TAURUS

You seek the truth solidly, stably, and through your physical senses. You learn through touch and make connections through contact. You want to ground your principles in the material world. You may idealize or over value money, possessions, pleasures, beauty or comfort. You could be independent in your approach to gratification and physical resources. You may be a risk-taker in handling income and outgo (believing you can always do more). You want financial independence.

**Examples:** *John Derek, Pancho Gonzales, Rip Torn, Morgana King, Sean Connery, Jim Jones, Omar Sharif, Bela Lugosi.*

### CHIRON IN GEMINI

You seek ideals through discussion, study and objectivity. You place a high value on thinking and communication. You easily adopt the role of student, teacher or traveler. You tend to be independent in your thinking and may be quite articulate. Probably a positive thinker, you find it easy to look ahead and seek out constructive answers.

**Examples:** *Bill Moyers, Elvis Presley, Herb Alpert, Lord Byron, Hugo Black, Alan Alda, Tom Smothers, Edmund G. Brown, Edna Ferber.*

### CHIRON IN CANCER

Your drive for enlightenment is emotionally based. You may idealize nurturing, protection, home, family, or roots. Yet, you may be restless in the nest, torn between freedom and security, or between valuing your home base and wanting to improve it — or sometimes, just to escape from its confinement. You probably value tenderness, compassion, caring and attachment. Emotional connections are a source of inspiration for you. Your quest for more understanding is focused on the arena of feelings, protection, preservation, home (or homeland), and family.

**Examples:** *Jerry Rubin, Jean Houston, Ringo Starr, Ryan O'Neal, Earl Warren, Ritchie Valens, David Frost, John Dean.*

## CHIRON IN LEO

The quest for the best is one you pursue lovingly, joyfully, and creatively. You may seek enlightenment through entertainment, speculation, taking risks, sex, love, or excitement. You can inspire others with your charisma and magnetism. You may want more than is possible from love, romance and sexuality. You may idealize children — or not have any because you can't raise them perfectly. You want to understand joy, drama and ego expansion. You are willing to experiment to expand your creative boundaries.

**Examples:** *John Lennon, Graham Nash, Muhammad Ali, Helen Reddy, Larry Flynt, Jimi Hendrix, Mick Jagger, Bruce Lee.*

## CHIRON IN VIRGO

You may seek the truth sensibly, pragmatically, methodically. Your quest for enlightenment can be practical; you are dedicated and hardworking in the pursuit of understanding. You might expect more than is reasonable in terms of work (perfect job, ideal colleagues, doing your work just right) or health, or strive to make a more ideal world. This could mean working hard to make the world conform to your ideals. You may go beyond traditional boundaries in your drive for efficient functioning.

**Examples:** *Robert De Niro, Herman Goering, Paramahansa Yogananda, Charlie Tuna (radio personality), John Denver, Hamilton Jordan, Duke of Windsor, Jean-Claude Killy.*

## CHIRON IN LIBRA

Your quest for enlightenment may be pursued gracefully, with beauty and balance or you could value competition. You may learn through others and teach much in relationships. You may idealize partners and partnership, perhaps expecting godlike perfection (from self or other) in relationships. Your restless urge for understanding affects the associations you choose.

**Examples:** *Franz Schubert, Jose Feliciano, J. Edgar Hoover, Henry Winkler, Diane Keaton, Lotte von Strahl, Suzanne Somers, F. Scott Fitzgerald.*

## CHIRON IN SCORPIO
Your quest for answers may be pursued with intensity and depth of purpose. You may find truth through cathartic or transformative experiences. You may idealize sexuality, intimacy, psychological insight, or power — perhaps expecting more than is reasonable from mates or from yourself in terms of mastery. You want to get to the bottom of issues involving morality, ethics and principles. Learning to share power or use it wisely may be a lesson.
   **Examples:** *O.J. Simpson, Uri Geller, Larry Csonka, Prince Charles, Arlo Guthrie, Arnold Schwarzenegger, Honore de Balzac, Lew Alcindor.*

## CHIRON IN SAGITTARIUS
Eager and enthusiastic for learning, you can pursue knowledge with humor. Ethical issues, moral principles and philosophical quests could be quite important to you. Your search for answers is geared toward Final Truth, toward absolutes. You may place a high value on honesty, the intellect, travel, science, expansion or anything that broadens your mental, physical, or spiritual horizons.
   **Examples:** *Vida Blue, Fred Astaire, Alexandre Dumas, Phoebe Snow, James Hilton, Victor Hugo, Adlai Stevenson, Enrico Fermi.*

## CHIRON IN CAPRICORN
Your drive for ultimate meaning may become a professional choice. You could work in a field involving education, publishing, travel, enlightenment, fun, or any kind of expansive, seeking effort. You can be quite responsible in your quest for answers about the meaning of the universe. You tend to take moral and ethical principles seriously. You might overrate power or power figures. You may be dedicated or hardworking in your pursuit of knowledge.
   **Examples:** *Hector Berlioz, Christopher Reeves, Henry Cabot Lodge, Benjamin Disraeli, Oscar Wilde, Hans Christian Andersen, Johnny Weismuller, Ralph Bellamy.*

## CHIRON IN AQUARIUS
Your quest for enlightenment is apt to be individualistic. You probably place a high value on tolerance, openness, freedom and/or equality. Your thinking may be original, inventive, and unusual — or strange, erratic and rebellious. Your principles and values are apt to differ a bit from convention. You enjoy going beyond traditional boundaries for information and answers.
   **Examples:** *George Bernard Shaw, Nikola Tesla, Sigmund Freud, Abraham Lincoln, William Saroyan, Simon Wiesenthal, Jean-Paul Sartre, William Jennings Bryan.*

## CHIRON IN PISCES

You may seek knowledge intuitively, through emotional openness. You could absorb wisdom and understanding. You tend to value sensitivity and compassion. You are likely to be idealistic — seeking the best and the highest in life. Developing a firm faith in something Higher in life will be a major asset for you. Mystical experiences are possible. Teaching, creating beauty, healing, and helping others may have great appeal.

**Examples:** *Giuseppe Verdi, Roy Rogers, Alan Watts, W.B. Yeats, John Galsworthy, Henri Matisse, Jacques Cousteau, Arturo Toscanini.*

## CHIRON IN ASPECTS

The following orbs are used in aspect examples: six degrees for conjunction or opposition; four degrees for square, trine or sextile.

## CHIRON CONJUNCT SUN

Creativity is marked in your nature. You are likely to seek admiration and attention for your ideas or ideals. You value (perhaps too much) recognition, acclaim, positive feedback. You may gain center stage through educating, inspiring, or informing people. You might persuade or lead others in terms of spiritual, ethical or moral principles. You could enjoy the expansion and excitement of travel or any grand schemes. Restlessness is highlighted, so be sure the activities you choose have enough variety, movement and intellectual challenge. You want to be noted as the very, very best!

**Examples:** *Jean-Claude Killy, Raphael, Willie Mays, Henry Mancini, Marlon Brando.*

## CHIRON HARMONY SUN

Your restless, curious, seeking and searching side could be one path to recognition. You may achieve leadership through moral and ethical principles, through educational or training efforts, through your persuasive skills or any actions which expand people's horizons or get them "up" and excited. Enthusiasm is one of your talents and you can be a skilled motivator. Your ambitions are apt to be high; you may occasionally expect more than is reasonable or feel let down by the "ordinary" in life. Generally, however, you bring much enterprise, mental eagerness, and charisma to your desire to reach the top.

**Examples:** *Alan Watts, Sidney Poitier, Rollo May (sextiles). Auguste Rodin, Earl Warren, Vida Blue, Albert Camus, Alan Alda, Bruce Lee (trines).*

## CHIRON CONFLICT SUN

Creative, eager, enthusiastic and excited, you can be a real ball of fire! Persuasive skills are likely with a talent for highlighting and accenting the best in yourself and others. Occasionally, idealism or too much perfectionism will lead you to be dissatisfied by the "real" (work-a-day) world. You could overreach, try to do too much, take chances, or risk your reputation for your principles. You can, however, be a great leader, a natural salesperson or persuader, and a fun-loving teacher, trainer, or promoter. You naturally shine in the realm of information and ideals.

**Examples:** *Jack London, Louis Pasteur, Dr. Tom Dooley, Johannes Kepler, W.B. Yeats (squares). George Bernard Shaw, Alfred Tennyson, Henry Cabot Lodge, Johnny Carson (oppositions).*

## CHIRON CONJUNCT MOON

You are apt to place a high value on home, your homeland, nurturing or meeting the needs of the public. This could lead to expecting more than is possible from your mother (figure), your family, or your own skills as a nurturer. You may want to be the perfect parent of perfect children — or decide, "If I cannot do it perfectly, I won't do it at all." You are likely to nurture thinking, exploring, and seeking in your family and might emphasize education for your children.

Another choice is a patriotic emphasis — idealizing the homeland through military work, public service, politics, etc. Or, you could provide basic needs (e.g., food, shelter, clothing) to people. You can be quite creative and insightful in reading public trends.

Your own home may be full of books, foreigners, intellectual discussions, philosophical arguments, speculation, or any form of expanding mental and physical horizons. A home in another country is also possible.

**Examples:** *Martin Luther, Paul Verlaine, William Jennings Bryan, Konrad Adenauer, Immanuel Kant, Victor Hugo, Richard E. Byrd.*

## CHIRON HARMONY MOON

You can blend roots and faraway places. This might lead to import-export activity, making people feel "at home" in the travel business, or other forms of combining the familiar with the lure of adventure.

You might be skilled at inspiring the public — through education, religion, metaphysics or another idealistic platform. You can get people to believe in what you value and pursue as long-range goals.

You are able to combine roots and adventure, so can have a stable home, but not be tied to it. You can enjoy saving, preserving and protecting as well as exploring, wandering and learning. Your mother figure could have contributed to your beliefs and values. Your ideas may charm the public or your emotional support can encourage others to learn more and to expand their horizons.

**Examples:** *O. Henry, Upton Sinclair, Bill Moyers, Roy Rogers (sextiles). Willie Mays, Wolfgang Mozart, Burt Reynolds, Wilt Chamberlain (trines).*

## CHIRON CONFLICT MOON

Idealism and compassion are highlighted, but you may be unsure how or where to channel them. Your quest for the best (the highest) may clash with your desire for safety and security. You may be unsure when to put down roots, and when to go on the road. Your values and ethical principles might have clashed with a nurturing figure. Your drive for freedom and individual expression could compete with your desire for a home, family, and a nest. You want to spread beliefs, moral principles, education or some kind of broadening, inspiring message to the public — or at least to your own home and family. You could be politically active, an idealist about nurturing, or seek adventurous safety (and safe explorations).

**Examples:** *Tom McLoughlin, John Glenn, Erwin Rommel, Robert Redford (squares). Muhammad Ali, Robert McNamara, Henry Cabot Lodge, Henry Kissinger (oppositions).*

## CHIRON CONJUNCT MERCURY

Curiosity is rampant in your nature. You want all the answers to all the questions in the universe. This could draw you into education, religion, travel, writing, journalism or anything which is mind-expansive. You thrive in an atmosphere of intellectual challenge and variety, and may have quite a quick wit and good sense of humor. You are likely to put a high value on logic, rationality, objectivity and intellectual understanding. You tend to put your faith in the mind.

Somewhat restless, you could have trouble settling down in life or work unless your position allows for movement, change and mental stimulation. Both depth and breadth of thought are highlighted. You are likely to feel driven to pursue knowledge and may be particularly concerned with issues of morality and the meaning of life.

**Examples:** *Benjamin Disraeli, Immanuel Kant, F. Scott Fitzgerald, Leonardo Da Vinci.*

## CHIRON HARMONY MERCURY

Ideas and ideals are highlighted by this combination. Your mind may fly in many different directions, with a wide range of interests likely. Anything involving intellectual stimulation, ethical and moral principles, or the freedom to travel or seek new horizons is possible. You are apt to have high standards and may sometimes want more information, more answers, or more variety than is possible in life. Your mind is a primary asset and should be used constantly.

**Examples:** *Alan Watts, Jack Paar, Orson Welles, Enrico Fermi, Jules Verne, Rollo May, Machiavelli (sextiles). Peter Sellers, William F. Buckley, Gustave Flaubert, Martin Luther, Upton Sinclair, Alan Alda (trines).*

## CHIRON CONFLICT MERCURY

An active, restless and eager mind is suggested. Your intellectual skills could be an asset in many different circumstances. Your curiosity about meaning and truth might lead you toward education, science, spiritual or religious paths, broadcasting, law courts or other idealistic or ethical pursuits. Your interest in freedom and desire for variety could pull toward travel or anything which allows you to keep on learning something all the time. You may sometimes want more than is possible in terms of understanding, or seek perfection where it does not exist. You may demand all the right answers from yourself. Your values could sometimes be in conflict with the people around you, or with society's traditions. If they are not overdone, your eagerness to learn and to explore are strong assets.

**Examples:** *Konrad Adenauer, Stephen Foster, Hugo Black, Edna Ferber, John Glenn, Jacques Cousteau, Carl Sandburg, Jimi Hendrix (squares). Muhammad Ali, H.G. Wells, R.D. Laing, Jack Anderson, Lenny Bruce (oppositions).*

(If you do not use the asteroids, also read the delineations for Chiron to Juno/Pallas as Chiron/Venus.)

## CHIRON CONJUNCT VENUS

Income (and outgo) could be tied to books, educational materials, inspirational (spiritual, philosophical, religious) matters, travel, law courts, journalism, or anything involving expansion (mentally or physically) or idealism. Enlargement of resources is one option which can range from making lots of money to dreaming (and not doing) about "when my ship comes in." You could idealize beauty, comfort, resources and pleasure — or put all your assets into the pursuit of a dream, a vision. Visualizing skills are likely. Plan for the future; this combination highlights the importance of the long-range view.

**Examples:** *Raphael, Hector Berlioz, Pancho Gonzales, Pere Teilhard de Chardin, Arthur Ashe, Hugh Downs, F. Scott Fitzgerald, Copernicus.*

## CHIRON HARMONY VENUS

Intellectual hunger could contribute to your financial base. Your restless, seeking, searching mind is apt to be a vocational asset or bring you a sense of comfort, stability, or pleasure. Your continual quest for more knowledge, inspiration, and information could be turned toward money-making or be a source of gratification. Income through ideas and/or ideals is implied (or idealizing money, possessions, pleasure, or beauty). Choose pursuits which give you freedom of movement, variety and a chance to keep on learning.

**Examples:** *Carl Sandburg, Rollo May, Glen Campbell, Ritchie Valens, Jack London, John Glenn, Karl Marx, Jerry Rubin (sextiles). Arlo Guthrie, Upton Sinclair, Honore De Balzac, David Frost, Helen Reddy, Sir Winston Churchill, Albert Schweitzer (trines).*

## CHIRON CONFLICT VENUS

Expectations are an issue in your financial picture or your search for pleasure. The possibility exists of hitting the big time monetarily, but another option is chronically dreaming (with no results) or wanting more than is possible. The key is backing up your talent for visualizing the best (which is highlighted) with realistic hard work. Follow up that inspiration with some perspiration! Talents already on your side include an independent spirit, mental restlessness that thrives on questions, and an urge to expand your horizons and potentials. You are learning to ground your visions, to put dreams into a practical, sensible form.

**Examples:** *Bruce Lee, Peter Fonda, Liberace, Joe Frazier, Adlai Stevenson (squares). Philip Berrigan, George Bernard Shaw, H.R. Haldeman, Graham Nash (oppositions).*

## CHIRON CONJUNCT MARS

You have an instinctive reach for more freedom, truth, meaning, understanding, knowledge and inspiration in life. This could lead you toward fields involving education, information dissemination, ethics, beliefs, travel, or anything that is broadening and expands your horizons. You may be a perpetual seeker — or identify with the truth and try to assertively convince others that your beliefs are **the** correct ones. You could be competitive or forceful about principles.

You can be quite a maverick, willing to pioneer, to take risks, to choose an unconventional path. Your energy and enthusiasm could be quite high; you are probably optimistic. You thrive on challenges and can respond quickly with whatever information or action is needed. You may be physically as well as mentally quick. You could overvalue assertion, or put too much faith in yourself, wanting everything on your own terms. Naturally curious, you will tend to seek more and more answers. Somewhat restless, you do best in an environment which allows you movement, variety and new mountains to conquer.

**Examples:** *Bill Moyers, Paul Newman, John Derek, Jean Cocteau.*

## CHIRON HARMONY MARS

Your quick curiosity could be an asset in life. Your quest for more meaning or information or understanding may help you to grasp concepts rapidly. Physical vitality, dexterity and good coordination are also possible. You usually act in harmony with your ideals and values, knowing what you want and going after it. You may have good instincts for just doing the "right" thing. With mental restlessness highlighted, you thrive in an environment of movement, change and intellectual stimulation. Freedom is accented, with an eagerness to move forward, pioneer and do what you want.

**Examples:** *Larry Csonka, Charlie Tuna (radio personality), John Lennon, Dean Martin (sextiles). Fred Astaire, William Blake, Arthur Ashe, Jon Voight (trines).*

## CHIRON CONFLICT MARS

Your quick mind could be an advantage in life. Because restless curiosity is highlighted, you need some movement and variety. You may sometimes act against your better judgment, when impulses or risk-taking drives predominate. Competitive instincts could clash with ideals and values, until you find a middle ground. Expectations might be an issue. You may want more than is reasonable — of yourself, or in areas of moral and ethical principles. A tendency toward high standards is suggested, but if you overidentify with the absolute, you might believe you already have all the answers (guru tendencies). You could clash with others around issues of values, beliefs and morality. The challenge is to be yourself, getting what you want in life without demanding superhuman perfection **or** trying to play God, believing that you have a right to whatever you want.

You could be drawn toward interest in education, information collection or dissemination, ideals and ethics, truth and meaning, travel, or anything which expands people's physical, mental, emotional, or spiritual horizons.

**Examples:** *Alan Alda, Percy B. Shelley, Immanuel Kant, Jim Jones (squares). Marcel Proust, Sir Winston Churchill, Jonathan Winters, David Frost (oppositions).*

## CHIRON CONJUNCT JUPITER

Idealism is highlighted in this combination. The quest for an absolute is quite strong in your nature. Note particularly the house (and sign) placements of Jupiter and Chiron.

It is likely that you will value education, religion, philosophy, travel, sports, exploration, speculation, or anything which is expansive and gives you a sense of higher meaning or knowledge. You could overvalue learning, science, or a particular set of beliefs and end up disappointed. Watch where you put your faith, lest you overdo and carry it to an extreme — or expect godlike perfection from a part of life that is limited. You may be strongly drawn to the roles of student and teacher. You are likely to be optimistic, with an eager enthusiasm for the future and a tendency to believe that the best is yet to come. A sense of humor could be quite marked.

**Examples:** *George Peppard, Henry Winkler, Jose Feliciano, Oscar Wilde, Diane Keaton.*

## CHIRON HARMONY JUPITER

Your intellectual values are likely to be compatible. You tend to be in inner agreement where matters of philosophy and ultimate meaning are concerned. Your leanings in regard to spirituality, religion, ethics, and morality tend to reinforce one another. Although you can be quite a seeker, a student of knowledge — and an eager disseminator — you are generally in tune with yourself in terms of long-range goals and significant values. Optimism, humor, a good ability to visualize the future, speculative urges and a pioneering mind are all possible.

**Examples:** *Muhammad Ali, F. Scott Fitzgerald, Bob Dylan, Jim Jones, Dr. Tom Dooley, H.G. Wells, James Dean, Albert Camus (sextiles). Marlon Brando, Vincent Price, Henry Mancini, Edmund G. Brown, Jerry Rubin, Ellen Burstyn (trines).*

## CHIRON CONFLICT JUPITER

You may feel some ambivalence about your beliefs and values. Perhaps you are so busy searching for answers, you have not really settled on anything yet. Perhaps you are convinced that the truth is always tentative. Perhaps you are torn in different directions in regard to moral, ethical, or spiritual principles. You may be attracted to the role of teacher and preacher — or student and seeker. A value hierarchy and practice at making priorities conscious can clarify your ideals. You might have too much faith, too little faith, or faith in the wrong area (e.g., expecting infinite satisfaction from a relationship, a person, a job, a bank account or some other limited part of life). Humor can be an important lightener in your life. Focus on what you want and trust and you can create more inner agreement rather than conflict. Compromise can help resolve conflicts between different goals and values.

**Examples:** *Marcel Proust, Percy Shelley, John Cage, Duke of Windsor, Albert Speer, William F. Buckley, Peter Fonda (squares). Sandy Koufax,*

*Giuseppe Verdi, Wolfgang Mozart, Thomas Mann, Jack Kerouac, Sir Winston Churchill, Alan Alda (oppositions).*

## CHIRON CONJUNCT SATURN

Variety, freedom, ideals and intellectual stimulation are highlighted for your career. This could range from the self-employed, solo operator, or unconventional worker to the free soul who doesn't want to settle down to one job. It could include fields involving information collection or dispersal, teaching, preaching, working for a better world. You may have high standards for yourself as a worker and for the contribution you wish to make to society. This can range from seeking the perfect job, trying to do your work without making any mistakes, turning the work ethic into a supreme value, or laboring to create a more ideal world. You need a sense of challenge, openness and mental activity on the job.

Your beliefs and values are likely to be strongly influenced by a father (or authority) figure. You might worship power, or place a high value on achievement. You could be somewhat conventional in your morality or world view, or you may be very serious and responsible where matters of ethics and principle are concerned. You tend to put your trust in hard work. You want to bring your beliefs down to earth and put them to work in the world.

**Examples:** *Walt Whitman, Prince Albert, Benito Mussolini, Rockwell Kent.*

## CHIRON HARMONY SATURN

Your path to success could be enhanced by additional training, studying, education, travel or application of moral and ethical principles. The focus is on idealism, sticking to principles, and gaining increased knowledge in order to achieve more success, status and accomplishments in life. Whatever stimulates you mentally has the potential of contributing to your career. You may be good at visualizing long-range goals and then breaking them into logical, practical steps. Both enthusiasm and the confidence to begin as well as the perseverance to finish up are emphasized.

**Examples:** *Jacques Cousteau, Maurice Ravel, Thomas Mann, Albert Schweitzer (sextiles). Dean Martin, Arturo Toscanini, Eduoard Manet, Jack Paar, Edwin Aldrin (trines).*

## CHIRON CONFLICT SATURN

Your challenge is to bring together regulations and freedom, ideals and practicality. Feeding the conflict could bring chronic frustration — the work is never good enough, doesn't pay enough, is too boring — or too risky —

or just not quite ideal. Or, you might give up on your dreams, afraid to try. You could feel torn between following the rules, fitting into the structure versus trying an alternative path and making changes. If you combine the principles successfully, you can have an original and creative sense of order and structure. You can have freedom within practical boundaries. You can be true to your vision and yearning for something more, yet pursue it with practicality and common sense, working voluntarily with "the rules of the game." With integration, your inventiveness, ethics and thirst for knowledge will become significant vocational assets.

**Examples:** *David Bowie, Willy Brandt, John Paul I, Evel Knievel, Wilt Chamberlain, Mark Spitz, Burt Reynolds, Phoebe Snow (squares). Leonardo Da Vinci, Jack Anderson, Steve Allen, William Jennings Bryan, Henry Kissinger (oppositions).*

## CHIRON CONJUNCT URANUS

Individuality, freedom, inventiveness and originality are highlighted. Restlessness (physical and mental) is likely. You may have a hard time staying in one place, ever ready to move, to look over the horizon, to seek more answers. You may be willing to take risks, speculate for greater gain. Creative thinking is quite likely; brainstorming could be a real talent. You can approach the mental realm from a different angle than most people.

Eager for independence, you are likely to guarantee yourself an available "escape hatch" at all times. You dislike being hemmed in, pinned down, or tied down. Rebelliousness or unconventionality might be carried to an extreme, or you simply march to a different drummer, finding your own path in life. You tend to put your faith in independent action. You place a high value on personal liberty.

**Examples:** *Ernest Hemingway, Billy Rose, Fred Astaire.*

## CHIRON HARMONY URANUS

Mental alertness and inventiveness are likely. You may pick up concepts more rapidly than most people. Ideas erupt constantly into your consciousness — some quite unusual. You can be a rebel in your thinking (but not necessarily in actions). The freedom to pursue knowledge and understanding is vital. Confinement is anathema to you. You will resist bonds and boundaries. You are likely to value democracy, justice, fair play and equality. You may be involved with idealistic or humanitarian causes. Your goals probably support intellectual stimulation, individuality and inventiveness.

**Examples:** *Johann Goethe, Bob Dylan, Ringo Starr, Peter Fonda (sextiles). Oscar Wilde, Arthur Rimbaud, Charles Watson, Konrad Adenauer, Henry Winkler (trines).*

## CHIRON CONFLICT URANUS

Clashes over individuality are possible. Perhaps you rebel against the ideals or beliefs of others. Perhaps your principles are revolutionary or unusual. Perhaps your drive for freedom comes out in a rash or erratic manner. Or, you may simply be very bright, quick, and determined to live on your own terms. Independence may matter much to you. Uniqueness may be an article of faith — something you value most highly. Intellectual stimulation and curiosity are accentuated.

**Examples:** *Jack London, Dr. Tom Dooley, Vincent Price, J. Edgar Hoover, Guy Ballard, Arnold Schwarzenegger, Vincent Van Gogh, W.B. Yeats (squares). George Bernard Shaw, Graham Nash, Johnny Carson, David Carradine (oppositions).*

## CHIRON CONJUNCT NEPTUNE

Idealism is doubled with this placement. You are likely to place a high value on the quest for meaning, inspiration and enlightenment. You could be drawn to beauty and aesthetics, to helping and healing, or to anything which gives people a glimpse beyond this physical plane. You may put your faith in the artistic or the inspired. Cosmic imagery is quite possible; you can visualize the big picture. Transcendence is a major goal. You want to be uplifted by life — and to share that mystical experience with others.

**Examples:** *Jose Feliciano, Upton Sinclair, Albert Einstein, Hermann Hesse, Carl Sandburg, Sir Alexander Fleming.*

## CHIRON HARMONY NEPTUNE

Harmony is suggested between your intellectual and emotional goals. Your head and heart may be in sync, with your mental beliefs and values supported by your intuition and inner wisdom. A mystical, idealistic, religious, philosophical, or transcendent focus is likely. Your quest for the ultimate may be overdone to the point of excessive imagination, escapism, or unreasonable perfectionism. Or, you may contribute to inspiring others through beauty, healing, helping, spiritual or rescuing activities.

**Examples:** *Vincent Van Gogh, Ringo Starr, Phoebe Snow, Arthur Rimbaud (sextiles). Ira Progoff, Philip Berrigan, Liberace, Daniel Berrigan, Harry Belafonte, Dr. Tom Dooley, William Blake, Paul Gauguin, Martin Luther, Raphael (trines).*

## CHIRON CONFLICT NEPTUNE
You may experience tension between different dreams and ideals. Your compassionate, tender, all-giving side may compete with your individualistic, independent, intellectual goals. You could feel torn between heart and head or intuition and logic. Your challenge is to take the best of both — to integrate the rational and nonrational. Idealism could be overdone, underdone, or channeled into the wrong areas — expecting too much of people, a job, possessions, etc. You are learning to consider your visions, to examine your dreams, and pursue the ones which appeal to you both mentally and emotionally.

**Examples:** *Gustave Flaubert, Zubin Mehta, Louis Pasteur, Glen Campbell, Walt Whitman, Karl Marx, Merle Haggard, Van Cliburn, Percy B. Shelley (squares). Karl E. Krafft, Enrico Fermi, Anatole France, Adlai Stevenson (oppositions).*

## CHIRON CONJUNCT PLUTO
You are likely to idealize or highly value sexuality, power, shared possessions, deep psychological understanding, or self-mastery. You may expect more than is possible from mates, or from yourself within an intimate association. You might worship intense emotional confrontations, catharsis, and transformations. You tend to trust depth, thoroughness, and perseverance.

**Examples:** *Prince Albert, Walt Whitman, Benito Mussolini, Karl Marx, Bruce Lee, Bela Lugosi, Bob Dylan, John W. Gacy, John Lennon.*

## CHIRON HARMONY PLUTO
Your urge for knowledge could enhance your handling of joint resources and pleasures. Your idealism, values, faith or confidence could contribute to intimate connections in your life. You and a mate may share goals, beliefs, inspiration or dreams and visions for a better future. Trust, world views, or moral and ethical principles could be significant issues with your closest partner(s). Your quest for enlightenment may encourage you to look deeper. You may seek and search by probing the depths of the psyche and uncovering hidden knowledge.

**Examples:** *Jim Jones, Sean Connery, Henry Winkler, Ellen Burstyn, Richard Alpert (Ram Dass), Hector Berlioz (sextiles). Eddie Albert, Wolfgang Mozart, Phoebe Snow, Honore de Balzac, J. Edgar Hoover, William Blake, Rollo May, Roy Rogers (trines).*

## CHIRON CONFLICT PLUTO
You may have a bit of reforming or revolutionary zeal. You are working on the integration of breadth and depth: wanting ultimate understanding of

everything, and wanting it on a deep level. You may feel torn between attachment versus separation, between maintaining an intimate connection with a mate versus accenting your freedom to explore, adventure and discover new ideas and ideals. Beliefs, values, or moral or ethical principles may be a bone of contention in relationships. You could clash with others over what is most significant and meaningful in life, or over expectations in relationships. Your challenge is to be true to your own intellectual hunger and need to know, while still able to relate closely with others.

**Examples:** *Mickey Rooney, Liberace, Nikola Tesla, George Bernard Shaw, Elton John, Jack Anderson, Dean Martin (squares). Martin Luther, Bruno Hauptman, Ernie Pyle, Raphael, Heinrich Himmler, Fred Astaire (oppositions).*

(For Ceres aspects, also include the sections of the Moon delineations which discuss mother figure.)

## CHIRON CONJUNCT VESTA OR CERES

Your work should include a sense of freedom, openness, variety and intellectual stimulation. Fields might range from inspiration (writing, publishing, metaphysics, philosophy) to education (teaching) to travel, technology or anything which enlarges people's perspectives. Your work might affect the wider world.

You may expect a lot of your career, or try to do it all perfectly. You may revere competence. An alternative is a high value placed on health and efficient bodily functioning. You'll be most satisfied with a job which helps to inspire or uplift people, or which expands their horizons and possibilities.

**Examples:** *Bill Moyers, Brooke Shields, Upton Sinclair, George Wallace (Ceres). Lord Byron, Michelangelo, Ellen Burstyn, Edna Ferber, Hugo Black, Walt Whitman (Vesta).*

## CHIRON HARMONY VESTA OR CERES

Your inventive, bright, problem-solving skills can be a real vocational asset. You need a job which stimulates your mind, provides an intellectual challenge, and reveals new possibilities and potentials to you and to the world. Variety is likely to appeal. A restless, seeking spirit is implied which needs to meet a high standard in the career. You want to do and be the best! Freedom of movement and action is your best bet in terms of professional environment. You could be a real pioneer as you are willing to try new paths and unconventional avenues in getting the job done.

**Examples:** *Vincent Van Gogh, Simon Wiesenthal, Peter Fonda (Ceres sextiles). Martin Luther, Omar Sharif, John Glenn, O. Henry (Ceres trines).*

*Dustin Hoffman, Peter Sellers, Abraham Lincoln (Vesta sextiles). Nikola Tesla, Van Cliburn, Richard Alpert [Ram Dass] (Vesta trines).*

## CHIRON CONFLICT VESTA OR CERES

You may be facing a challenge between idealism and realism or between wide-ranging interests versus focus. With the first, the main dangers are never being satisfied vocationally (searching continually for the "ideal" situation) or demanding more than is reasonable of yourself in terms of expertise and performance. Alternately, you may feel torn between a careful, precise focus on details versus a desire for variety, independence, risk-taking and intellectual stimulation on the job. A bit of both will work the best for you. Your mental acuity and innovative attitudes can provide a good balance to your dedicated desire for efficiency and careful analysis. You can do work that employs both your feeling for exactitude and your quest for intellectual challenges. You could rise to the role of expert in many areas.

**Examples:** *Lord Byron, Alfred Tennyson, Peter Sellers, John Lennon (Ceres squares). Arlo Guthrie, Johannes Kepler, H.R. Haldeman, Erwin Rommel (Ceres oppositions). Sigmund Freud, Jean Houston, Arthur Ashe, Edouard Manet (Vesta squares). Elton John, Henry Miller, Toulouse-Lautrec (Vesta oppositions).*

## CHIRON CONJUNCT PALLAS/JUNO

You may idealize relationships, a partner, or your role as a partner. You could expect more than is possible of marriage, try to be the "perfect" partner (perhaps as a guru or a savior), or look for your very own Prince/Princess Charming. You are likely to place a high value on beauty, grace, harmony and equality — or competition. You may attract partners who are mentally stimulating, spiritually searching, idealistic, willing to take risks, or fond of freedom. A passion for justice is possible. You may put your faith in compromise, charm, or cooperation.

**Examples:** *Orson Welles, Scott Carpenter, Herb Alpert, Oscar Wilde, Henri Matisse, Peter Fonda (Pallas). Hermann Goering, Paramahansa Yogananda, William Yeats, Stephen Foster, Vivien Leigh, Albert Camus, Glen Campbell, Diane Keaton (Juno).*

## CHIRON HARMONY PALLAS/JUNO

Your beliefs or ideals could contribute to your relationships. Your faith and confidence may make interactions with partners easier. You are likely to seek associates who are drawn to education, travel, science, spiritual quests, sports, speculation, or anything which is on the cutting edge or expands mental and/or physical horizons. You may seek out ways to create more justice and fair play in the world. You could put a priority on balance.

**Examples:** *Robert McNamara, Johnny Carson, Jean Houston, Jackie Robinson (Pallas sextiles). James Dean, Evel Knievel, John Dean, Nikola Tesla, Helen Reddy (Pallas trines). Omar Sharif, Alexandre Dumas, Burl Ives, Wilt Chamberlain, Victor Hugo (Juno sextiles). Johannes Kepler, Vida Blue, Jackie Robinson, Jean-Paul Sartre (Juno trines).*

## CHIRON CONFLICT PALLAS/JUNO

Issues around idealism, ethics, fair play, equality, social justice or values are likely in your associations with others. You may feel you have to fight for justice. Relationships which you want to be cooperative may become competitive. Your world view may differ considerably from a partner's. Moral conflicts or ethical dilemmas could arise. You may want more than is possible from your partner (or your partner may seem impossible to satisfy). You could be quite idealistic about relationships, equality, balance, harmony, beauty, or cooperation. You may apply your mind and originality to negotiation, aesthetics, or political action.

**Examples:** *Sigmund Freud, Henry Kissinger, Spiro Agnew, Walter Schirra (Pallas squares). Jack Kerouac, Steve Allen, John W. Gacy, Earl Warren (Pallas oppositions). Herb Alpert, Daniel Berrigan, Peter Ustinov, Vance Packard (Juno squares). Adolf Eichmann, Pere Teilhard de Chardin, Erwin Rommel, Dr. Sam Sheppard (Juno oppositions).*

## CHIRON CONJUNCT NORTH NODE

The quest for answers is built deep into your emotional foundation. You hunger for enlightenment and inspiration. You may overidealize in relationships, expecting godlike perfection from the people closest to you, or trying to "be everything" to those who depend upon you. Moral, ethical, philosophical, spiritual, and intellectual issues could be significant in your closest associations. You are torn between the freedom to pursue higher truth and the desire to connect emotionally with those around you. Your challenge is to make room for both caring and quests. You probably feel a strong attraction toward people who are bright, religious, idealistic, eager to travel, independent, ethical, honest, witty, or willing to take risks.

**Examples:** *Bobby Fischer, Jimi Hendrix, George Moscone, Jean Cocteau, Hans Christian Andersen, Maurice Ravel, Albert Schweitzer, Adlai Stevenson.*

## CHIRON CONJUNCT SOUTH NODE

The quest for higher truth is a karmic one for your lifetime. You may have to struggle to develop faith — perhaps going through a period of agnosticism or atheism. You may have too much faith — or trust in a limited part of life (turning money, a relationship, a person into "God"). You may do much questioning and seeking about ultimate answers and life's meaning. You will also face issues of freedom and idealism in relationships. It is essential that you allow space to your nearest and dearest, so you can all have freedom within commitment. You may expect too much from those who care about you, or those you look after. Your challenge is to be clear about values, beliefs, and priorities — both in terms of life's direction and also in terms of emotional commitments. And when you are clear, you can share your insights with others.

**Examples:** *Billy Carter, Michelangelo, Warren Beatty, Merle Haggard, Jack Kerouac, Jules Verne, Tom Smothers, Steve Allen.*

## CHIRON HARMONY NODES

Your ability to get close to others, to share emotional ties, is aided by your mental quickness, individuality, philosophical bent, or ethics and principles. Your desire for science, education, travel, or inspiration can be an asset in your relationships. You tend to associate with people who share your beliefs and values.

**Examples:** *Bertrand Russell, Hermann Hesse, Percy B. Shelley, Roy Rogers, Louis Pasteur, Bob Dylan, Hamilton Jordan ( North Node sextiles). Toulouse-Lautrec, Henri Matisse, Hermann Goering, Paramahansa Yogananda, Jean Houston, Van Cliburn, David Frost (North Node trines).*

## CHIRON CONFLICT NODES

Your ideals, values, beliefs, or faith may clash with those near and dear to you. You may have to face moral or ethical questions with close associates. You might feel that your quest for ultimate answers conflicts with your desire for relationships. Education, travel, science, philosophy, spiritual quests, or your dreams of something more may take you away from close contact with those you love — or vice versa. Your challenge is to make room in your life for both emotional and intellectual ties. You can clarify your faith and visions through sharing with others.

**Examples:** *Victor Hugo, Paul Cezanne, William F. Buckley, Albert Einstein (squares).*

## CHIRON CONJUNCT ASCENDANT

You seek to always know **more**. You are personally involved in a quest for perfection. You probably feel the urge to go beyond known boundaries — mentally and perhaps physically as well. You may naturally experiment/ take risks and could enjoy travel. You are likely to have significant freedom needs. Your mind may be sharp and quick, and your physical coordination above average. You could be a perpetual student and seeker — or a true believer willing to start religious wars on behalf of your principles. If you overidentify with your version of Truth, you could adopt a guru role. You might want more than is possible. You are apt to have high standards for your personal behavior — perhaps demanding too much on occasion. You are naturally optimistic. You need to find your own answers (beliefs).

**Examples:** *Fred Astaire, Rollo May, Vincent Price, Burt Reynolds, Paramahansa Yogananda, Mario Lanza, George Patton.*

## CHIRON HARMONY ASCENDANT/DESCENDANT

You may perpetually seek to know **more**. You might embark on a quest for perfection. You probably feel a drive to go beyond known boundaries. You can enjoy experimenting and trying new approaches/ideas. Your actions may aid or assist freedom. You might ask a lot of yourself. You can be a risk-taker. Ideals, beliefs or education may be helpful to you. Faith and self-confidence build your courage even more. You tend toward optimism. Trust and a belief in the meaning of life support your pioneering spirit. Your energy flows easily into learning/teaching or into body-training. Expanded horizons make you feel more alive. You may be restless with a need for variety. Progressive ideas stimulate you.

**Examples:** *Leopold Stokowski, Johnny Weismuller, William F. Buckley, Richard Alpert (Ram Dass), Tom Smothers, Jack Paar (Ascendant sextiles). Oscar Wilde, Isabelle Pagan, Sir Lawrence Olivier, Van Cliburn, Hal Holbrook, Lenny Bruce, Alexandre Dumas (Ascendant trines).*

## CHIRON CONFLICT ASCENDANT/DESCENDANT

A focus in the *now* may seem incompatible with a pull toward the future; make them work together. Freedom issues could be touchy for you; avoid the extremes of too much or too little. You might sometimes go overboard (or underboard) with experiments or risk-taking. You may be restless with an urge to travel. Expectations (too high or too low) are an important personal challenge. You may demand more than is possible of yourself. Intellectual stimulation energizes you. Ideals and aspirations might sometimes pull you away from taking care of yourself. Lifelong learning is important to you. Personal needs may conflict with an urge to know **more**. (Do some of each.) Personal action to gain attainable goals may compete with a quest for perfection; you can get what you want and still pursue a Higher Truth. Immediate desires may compete with your urge to go beyond known boundaries. Who you are may conflict with your expectations (who you "should" be). "Running away" may appeal when you feel tied down. You may clash with others over beliefs/values until you have a firm, but relaxed, sense of your own standards. You are learning how best to be true to yourself, without alienating close associates.

**Examples:** *Sam Peckinpah, Liberace, Ernest Hemingway, Nikola Tesla, William Blake, Jean-Paul Sartre, Orson Welles, Alan Watts (squares).*

## CHIRON CONJUNCT DESCENDANT

You might seesaw back and forth in satisfying your urge to know **more**. You may inhibit your actions with a quest for perfection (or believe you can do anything). You might overdo or underdo the urge to go beyond known boundaries. You might experience extremes in terms of experiments or risk-taking. High expectations could influence your partnerships. Freedom issues affect your relationships. You are attracted to people who stimulate your mind or who are idealistic. Your partnership(s) will be strongly affected by ideals, values and beliefs. You seek a sense of growth and expansion in your associations. You are apt to be restless, creative and progressive in partnerships.

**Examples:** *Brooke Shields, Henry Cabot Lodge, Albert Schweitzer, Upton Sinclair, Auguste Rodin, William Holden.*

## CHIRON CONJUNCT MC (MIDHEAVEN)

You may be drawn toward intellectual vocations (writing, teaching, computers). You are likely to prefer variety in your work. You can be quite independent in your approach to a career. You might idealize power, authority, the work ethic, or competence. You may be practical about your beliefs, values, and long-range goals. Your drive for power may be directed toward knowledge. You might travel or broaden people's horizons in your work. Your perception of reality is likely to be idealistic. You want your status to give you freedom. You may be willing to experiment/take risks to achieve success.

**Examples:** *Alfred Tennyson, Galileo, Richard Strauss, Paul Verlaine, Philip Berrigan, Nathan Leopold, Robert Stack.*

## CHIRON HARMONY MC/IC

Your willingness to take risks can enlarge your career success. Your idealism and belief in doing **more** may add to your status. Your attraction to far horizons could enrich your work. Your urge to know more may expand your power base. Your clear values may help you relate to authorities, handle power yourself, and integrate work and home. Your intellectual openness and idealism could enhance your status. Mentors may assist your ability to seek spiritual, metaphysical, and religious answers. Further training/education is likely to add to your success. Your high standards and quest for the best can increase your achievements. You have the capacity to blend idealism and realism, visions and pragmatism; career and family.

**Examples:** *Hector Berlioz, Henry Kissinger, Gustave Courbet, Ralph Bellamy, Jack Kerouac, Jack Nicholson, Jack London, Edmund G. Brown (sextiles to Midheaven). James Hilton, Burt Reynolds, Dr. Tom Dooley, Immanuel Kant, Rip Torn, Jacques Cousteau, Wilt Chamberlain, Louis Pasteur, Auguste Rodin (trines to Midheaven).*

## CHIRON CONFLICT MC/IC

Your need for variety may seem to interfere with productivity until you turn it into a vocational asset. Your interest in far horizons may clash with your desire for success or conventional security. Your power drive may seem at odds with your moral ethics and principles, or you might choose a career which accents morality or beliefs. Your risk-taking, experimental side may seem incompatible with authorities or with a stable home and family; find a middle ground. Spiritual, metaphysical or truth-seeking activities may compete with your desire to make a living. A quest for perfection can make work satisfaction difficult to achieve. Your intellectual desires may be at odds with the rules/roles of society. Your urge to go beyond the known may clash with the weight of traditions. Your freedom needs may seem incompatible with cultural limits/restrictions; do what you can within the structure of society. You are working on the balance between realism and idealism.

**Examples:** *John Dillinger, Muhammad Ali, Brooke Shields, Mario Lanza, Hugo Black, Marcel Proust, Albert Schweitzer, Earl Warren, Benito Mussolini, Dean Martin, Upton Sinclair (squares).*

## CHIRON CONJUNCT IC

You may place a high value on home and family, yet periodically leave home for far horizons. It may be a challenge to fit your beliefs and principles into society's demands. You may feel a need to integrate idealism and realism. It may seem difficult to get enough variety and mental challenges at work. Your desire to take risks could seem to take you away from authority positions. You may expect a lot from your family members (or they from you). The urge to go beyond known boundaries might pull you away from conventional success. You are likely to feel freedom versus closeness urges around your nest, or to feel pulled between family commitments and work obligations and ambitions. Your domestic environment could be very mentally stimulating. Spiritual understanding, independence, intellectual stimulation, or faith that everything will work out may be an emotional foundation in your life.

**Examples:** *Sean Connery, Henry Mancini, David Carradine, Spiro Agnew, Zubin Mehta, James Lovell, Ernest Hemingway, John Galsworthy, Bill Moyers.*

## CONCLUSION

May the themes of Chiron light your life with faith, confidence, the ability to take risks when appropriate, high ideals, and a world view which gives you a sense of meaning and purpose. May you enjoy the intellectual stimulation, humor, opportunities for travel, spiritual insights, and inspiration toward **more** — which Chiron represents.

The charts, reports and most books listed in *All About Astrology* booklets
are available through:
 Astro Communications Services, Inc.
 5521 Ruffin Road
 San Diego, CA  92123
 1-800-888-9983

© 1994 ACS Publications

ISBN 0-936127-24-0